Based on a

Magnificent Millie

WRITTEN BY
Stefanie Patterson

ILLUSTRATIONS BY
Caroline Robertson

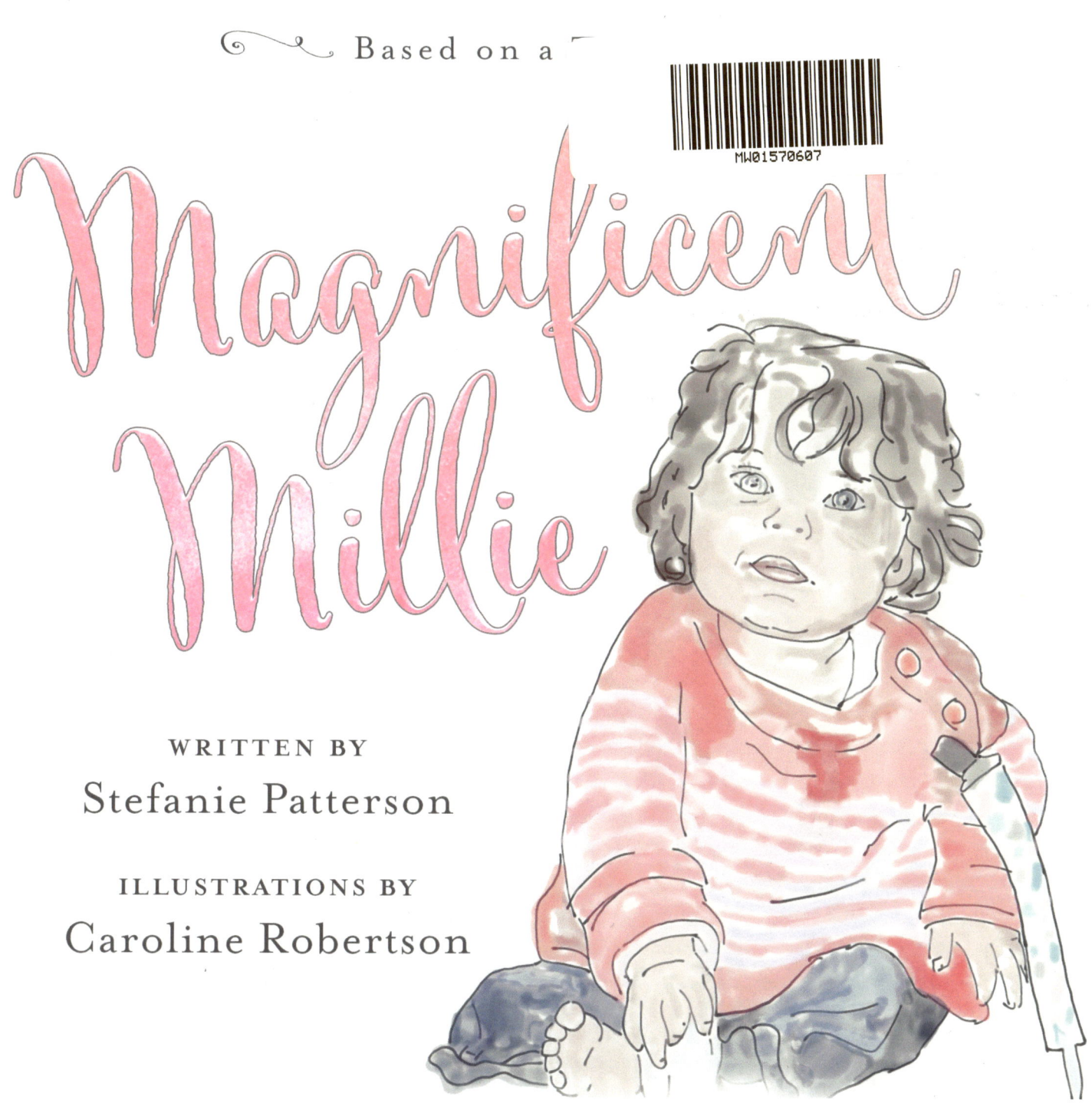

Fly high baby girl and know how much your family loved you.

Until we see you again in that place in the sky,

know we carry you with us in everything we do and everywhere we go.

You made a huge impact on this world in your short time.

You showed the world how to love and be strong.

Mama and Dada are incredibly proud of who you are.

Love you always,

our Baby Shark and Heart Warrior,
- Millie Grace Robertson

xoxoxoxo

"Love endures everything, love is stronger
than death, love fears nothing."

There is an extraordinary place where we all come from,
somewhere high up in the sky,
between the clouds and the stars.

We all come here from that place
with the hope of giving and receiving love.

For some of us, it takes a long time but for others,
it takes a short time.

When Millie came here,
her heart was only half the size of a regular heart.
It was tiny but mighty.

She spent many months at a Hospital
where Doctors and nurses with medical powers
and special medicine helped her tiny heart become strong.

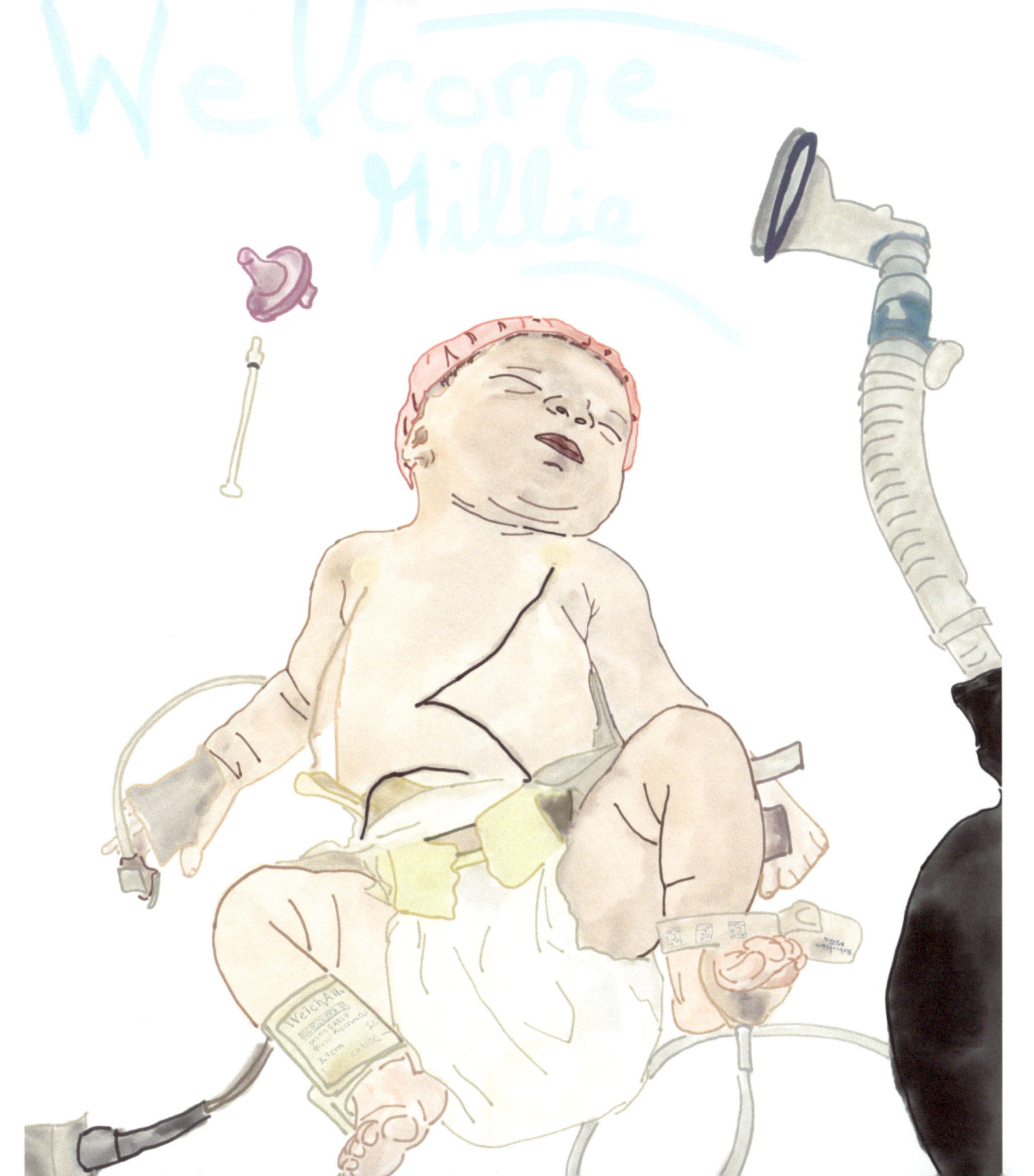

Millie was brave, tough and determined
to make her little heart well enough
to be able to fully give and receive love.

She had places to go and people she had to meet!

Millie began to smile, dance and laugh
while her Dada would hold her little hands all night long,
her Mama would sing sweet lullabies to her all day
and all her loved ones would cheer,
"Millie, you've got this!"

Magnificent Millie, look at how brave you are.

Over some time,
the Doctors and nurses with medical powers
and special medicine made Millie's tiny heart strong
enough for Millie to leave the Hospital and go home.

She spent hot summer days outside
feeling the warm sun on her skin,
listening to the birds tweet
and tasting the most delicious food.

As the seasons changed
and the leaves began to fall from the trees,
it was time for Millie to go back to the Hospital
where Doctors and nurses with medical powers
and special medicine needed to repair her tiny heart again.

Her Dada and Mama were worried but through
Millie's rising love, she assured them it was okay.

During many medical tests at the Hospital,
Millie continued to smile, dance and laugh
while her Dada continued to hold her little hands all night long,
her Mama continued to sing sweet lullabies to her all day
and all her loved ones continued to cheer,
"Millie, you've got this!"

Magnificent Millie, you have come so far.

The medical tests showed Millie's tiny heart was growing
well, so the Doctors and nurses with medical powers
and special medicine told her Mama and Dada
they could return home again.

All of Millie's loved ones were thrilled for the exciting
events they had planned for them when they got home.

Before long, it was Millie's First Birthday
and it was a grand celebration at home.

Loved ones celebrated from near and far.
Her and her tiny heart were miracles.

Everyone shouted with joy,
"Happy Birthday, Millie!"

After the grand cerebrations of her First Birthday,
it was that magical time of Christmas.

Millie went on sleigh rides in the snow,
wore beautiful dresses with bows and lace
and got a ton of presents from Santa.

Millie still smiled, danced and laughed
while her Dada would still hold her little hands all night long,
her Mama would still sing sweet lullabies to her all day
and all her loved ones would still cheer,
"Millie, you've got this!"

Magnificent Millie, we are so proud of who you are.

During all the fun,
her Dada and Mama knew Millie's tiny heart was getting tired.

Off they went, back to the Hospital
where Doctors and nurses with medical powers and
special medicine waited for them to arrive.

It was time to mend her tiny heart again.

Her Dada and Mama were concerned
but Millie's love made them smile.

Magnificent Millie, it's time to rest now amongst the stars.

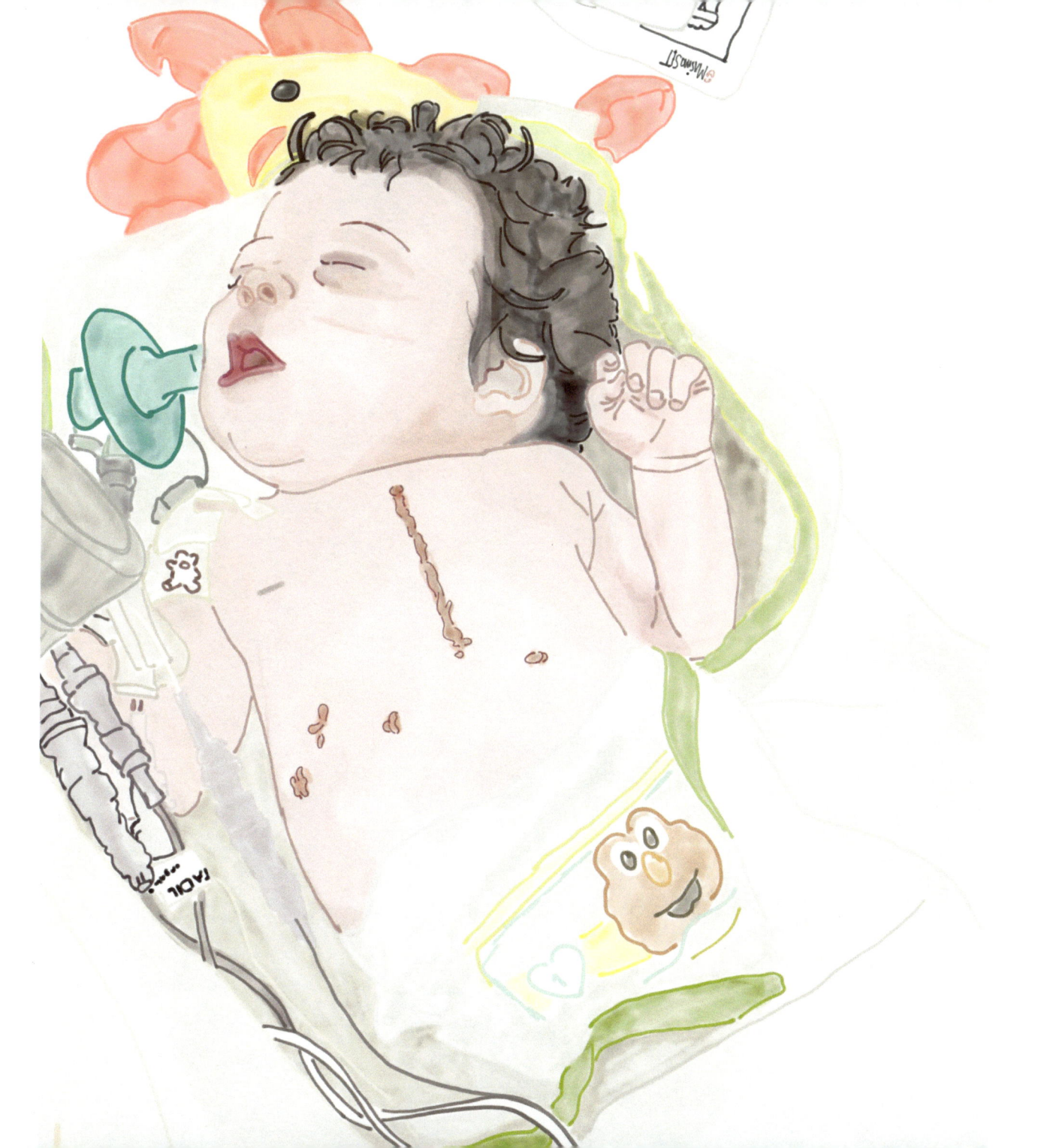

While she slept at the Hospital,
everyone knew Millie's time had come
for her to go back somewhere high up in the sky,
between the clouds and the stars.

The love she gave and had received was plenty
but, in fact, it was more…

Millie's loved ones were sad to let her go
but with every tear that fell,
a flower grew in its place.

As time went by, they would often
watch her paint the sunsets pink,
listen to her play music between the gentle waves in the ocean
and sometimes even feel her brush warm winds
against cold skin.

Even though her time here was short,
the love she had left continued to be seen, heard and felt.

Perhaps we will see Millie smile, dance and hear
her laugh in that extraordinary place in the sky
one day, but until then her love remains.
Magnificent Millie, here you are.

About the Writer

This is Stefanie's first Children's Book. Writing has always been her escape and now, it has a purpose. She resides in Bradford, Ontario with her husband (Jamie), two young children (Eleanor and Henry) and her English bulldog (Gus).

She and her family met Millie during Henry's stay at The Hospital for Sick Children in Toronto, Ontario, in early 2017, as her son, Henry, also has a congenital heart defect. He and Millie recovered along with other special Heart Warriors and their families after having open heart surgery as a newborn baby.

1 in every 100 babies are born with one or more congenital heart defects. Having a heart defect is a lifelong commitment, there is no cure.

These children are our heroes, we can all learn something from them.

About the Illustrator

Caroline is Millie's Mama.

Her and her husband (Derek) live in a beautiful century home in Yarmouth, Nova Scotia with their two labradoodles (Kirby and Ella). The four of them enjoy spending lots of time on the beach.

When Stefanie began the process of writing a Children's Book about Millie, Caroline knew she had to be part of the process. She loves drawing colourful and fun images, she also knew Millie's face and personality best.

Millie's family loved her more than anything in the world. She had so many special times at home. She was a true Heart Warrior.

Magnificent Millie

Copyright © 2018 by Stefanie Patterson

Written by Stefanie Patterson
Illustrations by Caroline Robertson

All rights reserved. No part of this publication may be reproduced, distributed, or transmitted in any form or by any means, including photocopying, recording, or other electronic or mechanical methods, without the prior written permission of the author, except in the case of brief quotations embodied in critical reviews and certain other non-commercial uses permitted by copyright law.

Tellwell Talent
www.tellwell.ca

ISBN
978-0-2288-0513-7 (Paperback)

CPSIA information can be obtained
at www.ICGtesting.com
Printed in the USA
LVHW07n0306060918
589327LV00001B/15/P